Waters of Cumbria

"and all the landscape endlessly enrich'd
With waters running, falling, or asleep."

William Wordsworth, *The Prelude*

*This book is dedicated to the many people who have
encouraged me by their support and interest in my work,
in particular the great patience shown by
Mole, Lool, Sticky and Light.*

WATERS of CUMBRIA

David Herrod

CREATIVE
MONOCHROME

WATERS OF CUMBRIA
by David Herrod
with foreword by Colin Welland

Published in the UK by Creative Monochrome
20 St Peters Road, Croydon, Surrey, CR0 1HD.

British Library Cataloguing-in-Publication Data:
A catalogue record for this book is available
from the British Library.

ISBN 1 873319 13 4
First edition, 1994

Printed in England by The Bath Press, Lower Bristol Road,
Bath, Avon, BA2 3BL.

Foreword

Colin Welland

The lure of the Lakes is hard to pin down. Ever since I first arrived amidst its fells at the age of fifteen, I've been haunted by its presence. I like to feel it awaited my return year after year; but rather it was *I* who longed to go back. It probably wasn't even aware of my existence – any of our existences.

And yet Wordsworth suspected it was. More than that, he believed it felt paternal towards to us: guarding, guiding, chastising, comforting, inspiring those who fall beneath its spell.

For the Lakes is a presence, a being, a reality which has been so for millions of years. To stand on its massive, rolling, slumbering back is a privilege: a timeless experience shared by brooding fellow dreamers way down the centuries.

I remember driving through Cumbria when the kids were small and fractious. "Look at the scenery," we said. "What *is* scenery?" they asked, and they were right. The scenic movement which built the railway, brought the hordes, sells the cream teas, buys the coloured postcards, packs the roads with cars and the fields with caravans, simply got it all wrong. The Lakes is not about looking pretty, it's about being bold, aggressive, angry and dangerous ... or calm, breathless and still. It's about changing light and sweeping rain; thunderheaded peaks and yawning, cavernous gaps; aching hush and icy stillness; and bracken bristling in the heavy summer heat.

In other words, it's about mood.

Yet it's this mood which has evaded artists since the Lakeland was popularly discovered two hundred years ago. Turner, the master of atmosphere, caught it momentarily, then, yearning for Chelsea, caught the next train home. Constable flicked a fleeting bristle, but found it all too much, preferring the lush foliage, the clumping cattle and the tinkling waters of East Anglia. It's strange how the glowering hills and roaring ghylls found soaring expression through the pens of romantic poets, but were failed by those whose genius lies behind their eyes.

Painfully aware of this, I've tramped the local galleries searching for one soulmate whose brush captures what Cumbria means to me – but all to no avail. Perhaps a sculptor's feel is needed – like the rolling, slumbering forms of Henry Moore. The milky insipidity of water colourists can't stand the heat, and the tricksy skills of Lakeland artists, well established in popular demand, fail their subject miserably: like playing Wagner on a pianola.

Lithographs can work: the bold, stark strictures of the medium suiting the simple majesty of the ancient waters and fells, but it was in photography where I found salvation.

David Herrod joins a distinguished line of cameramen to whom we Lakes lovers owe an everlasting debt. Don't ask me why they have succeeded where painters failed, but succeed they have, and to a wonderful effect.

Again I suspect the simple restrictions of the early techniques lent themselves to the sometimes fleeting magic which is Cumbria's own, and, despite all the paraphernalia now available, the best of the modernists approach their work with the same uncluttered directness as their forebears.

Herrod is like that; snapping away apparently merrily, and yet his half-closed eyes already see way beyond the shot, completing the process and conceiving the grandeur in pictorial terms before the shutter ever falls.

When in my Threlkeld home, over a coffee, he unfolded his portfolio, there at last were my lakes, spread out before me. That sunrise over Loweswater would leave old William gasping, "every icy crag tinkling like iron". "Up early for that one," David said. Up early, yes, but up with the inspired knowledge that that magic mood would be there to capture, and, most important of all, with the wonderful certainty that the shimmering miracle would be worth the effort.

David Herrod loves the Lakes. Through his camera, he lays that love down before us in black and white. He caresses his prints with an almost paternal care and affection, knowing that contained in them is his solemn conviction as to what life and its living is all about.

As you turn these pages, you're privileged to share that conviction. Bask in it. And then go, yourselves; go to sit and ponder on your own intimations of immortality beside those still, eternal waters which are the Lakes.

Colin Welland
January 1994

The magic brew

Although Cumbria is the second largest county in England, with an area of approximately 2600 square miles, it is better known to many people by the name given to its central area – The Lake District – even though this only represents about one-third of the total area of the county.

The name, The Lake District, is self-descriptive, but to make a fine point, of the many tracts of water collected together here, only one of them is actually called a lake: the others are called meres or waters. Hair-splitting aside, these lakes and all the attendant rivers, streams and ponds, combine harmoniously with the surrounding countryside to form an area of outstanding natural beauty.

The water has many guises – lakes, tarns, pools, rivers, becks, trickles, mist, cloud, rain, ice and snow. Each property has a character of its own. Mix these with the wide range of topographical features of the area and you have a magic brew, one where every sample is different. The topography alone is unusual in that there is such a wide variety in such a compact area.

The complex geology plays an essential role in this, again with the vital involvement of water.

The area was once a sea, which collected the dust filling the air, during a very violent period in the Earth's formation. Successive layers of material deposited in enormous thicknesses caused great pressure, so that fine grained thinly layered rock was formed, named by geologists as Skiddaw Slate. Volcanic eruptions in the central area, now with such well known names as Scafell and Great Gable, caused great disruption. Then followed alternating periods of seas and deserts, depositing other material to form limestone and sandstone. Upheavals in the earth's crust disrupted these formations, folding them and thrusting them into huge mountain ranges with igneous intrusions into the Eskdale, Ennerdale and Buttermere areas, so that now we have formations of slate, limestone, sandstone, mixed volcanics and granite. After this violent activity, which went on over a period of five hundred million years, water again played its part.

The upward thrusting masses of rock present a barrier to moisture-laden winds, resulting in high rainfall and a continuing battle. The persistent attack of water has shaped the rocks and enhanced their characters. The softer rocks have been worn away and their contours smoothed, so that they contrast with the jagged intrusions of their harder neighbours. Cracks and folds have formed channels in which the water runs, cutting them deeper and wider to form gullies and valleys. The resulting silt and debris have dammed valleys to form the lakes. The finer particulate matter, blown by the wind, has acted as an abrasive and helped the water in its sculptural work. Then, in periods when the frozen water of the polar ice cap extended over this area, the crushing and gouging forces of immense masses of ice caused further shaping to the pattern.

We now have peaks, crags, slabs and screes. Where the particulate matter has settled, it supports vegetation in the form of heather, bracken, grass, trees and others too numerous to mention. The water itself is abundantly manifested in becks, rivers, tarns and lakes.

The generous presence of water and the fertile valleys have attracted human beings through the ages. Evidence of Neolithic man has been found in the stone axe workings on the Langdale Pikes and Scafell Pike. The most famous relic of Bronze Age man is the stone circle at Castlerigg near Keswick. An Iron Age fort existed on Castle Crag in Borrowdale, later taken over by the Romans, whose most impressive fort in the area is at the foot of Hardknott Pass. The Vikings settled in the area extensively and are responsible for many of the local place names, such as 'thwaite' (clearing), 'garth' (enclosure), 'fell' (hill), and 'beck' (stream). Then came the Normans, who encircled the area with castles and monasteries.

The rich mineral content of the volcanic material and the value of slate as a building material have encouraged mining and quarrying, some of which continues today. Every generation has left its mark. The landscape has been changed by customs and cultures: systems of farming, clearing woodland, cultivating and grazing; building structures and the thousands of miles of walls which march across fields and fells; and the buildings, by using indigenous materials, emphasising the geological diversities of the area.

This is the magic brew, but like all others, without water there would be nothing. Constantly moving in its own life cycle, it provides the lifeblood for everything else. It is a force to be respected, but at the same time admired. Even in its frozen state, when it appears to be in suspended animation, it has properties which in the right circumstances, can exert devastating forces on the hardest of rocks. In its angry moments, it brushes aside any attempt to control it and often makes us pay for our contempt. The residents of Upper

Borrowdale experienced this at first hand in the great flood of 1965. Whatever its mood, it has – for all ages – an attraction leading to fascination.

It reflects, distorts, ripples, sparkles, scintillates. It lies placid. It trickles, tumbles, rushes and roars. In its vaporous state, suspended in air, it restricts visibility in varying degrees with haze, mist, fog and cloud. In its crystalline state, as snow, it transforms everything: 'winter wonderland' may be a cliché, but is still the perfect description.

In all its many forms, it displays diverse moods and combines with the other elements of the landscape to create a further range of moods. This is probably the most important factor in creating the magic of The Lake District. The variety of moods is endless. Our disdain for our wet climate is known internationally, but how dull and boring the area would be with a constantly cloudless sky.

Until relatively recent times, the attractions of the area were enjoyed mainly by the people living here. When the writings of people such as William Wordsworth began to circulate, his contemporaries were attracted. Wordsworth is perhaps the prime example of one completely captivated by The Lake District magic. Born here, he was by no means parochial in his lifestyle, travelling widely at a time when this was not without its difficulties. But he could not find a match for his beloved Lake District and returned to spend the majority of his life here. His contemporaries and companions added their own praise. They basked in the magic and used it to fuel their own creativity to produce another magic – a spiritual one. This continues, generation after generation. Most of the works are romantic, some fictional, but all are inspired.

The intrepid travellers of Wordsworth's time came to see for themselves. Some were overawed and took back tales of wild, "horrid" scenery. This in itself may have been a further attraction rather than a deterrent. It was the advent of the railways which first brought the visitors in significant numbers and started the tourist trade. Now millions of visitors come every year to partake of the magic brew.

The principal value of water is, of course, its life-sustaining quality and it was this which attracted people to settle here. As the population grew, so did the demand for water, and many of the lakes and rivers provided the supply. Some, such as Crummock Water, Ennerdale Water and Wastwater, have had to be raised artificially, by only a few feet, to meet the local demand.

Other areas of England, not so well endowed, coveted the abundant supply and succeeded in gaining Government approval to siphon off vast quantities for themselves. To do this, artificial lakes have been created, vastly greater in size than nature provided.

Thirlmere, for instance, was originally two small lakes. In 1892, the City of Manchester built a dam to create one large lake. Similarly, in 1929, they built a dam to create Haweswater, raising the water level by nearly one hundred feet, flooding many fields and buildings in the process. In the 1960s, demand increased yet again and permission was obtained to abstract water from Ullswater.

The demand continues to grow. Because we have a plentiful supply of water, we have little respect for it. We abuse it and misuse it. If we lived in an arid climate, how different our attitude would be.

In areas of the country without large lakes, the underground aquifers are being pumped out faster than they are being filled. Rivers and streams are disappearing. Such actions will place greater demands on areas with an apparent abundance of surface water. There is talk of constructing a national grid pipe network.

Even now, the demand on the Waters of Cumbria takes its toll visually. With the fluctuations in water levels, ugly raw shorelines are exposed on those lakes where abstraction takes place and none more so than those which have been artificially raised, with the greatest demands.

In the worst cases, when there has been a period of low rainfall, the water levels of the artificial lakes have fallen so far that the forlorn remains of original buildings and structures, long since drowned, are revealed. To many, these revelations are nothing more than passing curiosities. Something to gape at and destroy in the mindless quest for souvenirs. However, our consciences should be pricked. The ugly expanses of raw boulders, mud and silt should jar our senses and make us think about what is happening. Without controls, better management, distribution and conservation, not only will a beautiful area be destroyed, but also the distant dependants will lose their lifeblood: a disaster for everyone!

We must take action to conserve the magic of the brew.

My photographs

My love of The Lake District began over forty years ago. I consider myself to be very fortunate to be able to live and work here; to see its many moods, which the visitor, whether casual or frequent, will be unlikely to experience. It has been said that a real love of The Lake District is due to feeling that everything is in harmony: a balance between all the elements of the landscape and all the forces acting upon them.

Many eloquent people have been able to express their feelings in poetry and prose; others in paint, music and other media. My attempt to communicate is through my photographs. They can speak my feelings better than I can put them into words.

With this set of photographs, I have tried to chronicle some of the many and varied aspects of water as it affects this area. I have featured some of the lakes several times, while others are not featured at all. The only significance in this is that I have chosen my favourites. The portfolio in no way pretends to be exhaustive.

I have tried to capitalise on the water's aesthetic qualities and thereby generate a wider empathy. Hopefully this will result in a more careful respect of this most important natural resource.

The sequence I have chosen is first to show the effect of the presence of water in the landscape where, although its proportion of the view is small, its significance is great. This significance grows as its scale increases and, with its greater prominence, some of its own properties are revealed. The camera moves progressively closer until, finally, water itself becomes the sole subject.

Every study attempts to be aesthetically satisfying as an individual image. I hope the images will give enjoyment to those people who appreciate The Lake District landscape and to those who find photography an exciting medium of the visual arts.

It is a disappointing fact that many people in Britain do not accept photography as an art form. It is seen as purely a technical exercise: something that anyone can do. Modern technology has increased the chances for the inexperienced of making a properly exposed photograph. If that is the only objective, then there is a strong chance of achieving success. But compare this to painting by numbers or the pianola's purely mechanical reproduction of written music. Are any such results likely to be hailed as works of art? If not, why not? Surely, it is because they have no spirit and convey no feelings. Any form of art must have these essential ingredients.

Photography is used to produce pictures, just as the use of paintbrushes, pencil, or any other marking medium does. If the resulting image generates feelings in the viewer, then I believe it is a work of art. The success depends on the eye and sensitivity of the creator and the skill by which the available tools and materials are used: in that order. Having good quality equipment certainly helps, but it is the photographer rather than the camera and lenses that determines the success of the image. It is demeaning to the photographer and a debasement of photography to assume that it would be otherwise.

Another factor which leads people to the view that photography is not art is the belief that photographic prints can be produced *ad infinitum*, each one identical to the others. This mass production is thought to trivialise or de-value photography. This seems to me not so much an appreciation of art as the mentality of the collector who equates value to scarcity. The idea of mass production is, in fact, ill-founded since fine prints usually require some degree of manipulation by hand at the printing stage, which can never be precisely replicated.

The medium of monochrome photography allows a greater latitude in this manipulative technique. This in itself gives the photographer a greater feeling of being in touch with his work and thus may be considered to be more expressive. I certainly find this so. I do also work in colour, but find greater satisfaction with monochrome, which is why I have chosen the medium for this collection.

My approach to photography could be termed spontaneous or intuitive. I am not a technician. My methods have been built up over many years of experience. I prefer to work with simple equipment of good quality, where I retain control over the settings. I do not worship equipment, nor do I drool over print quality. The photograph is the end product and conveying feelings through it is of the utmost importance to me. Definition, tonal range and the other factors which comprise print quality are desirable objectives, but not an end in themselves.

We seem to live in an era where only those images which shock our senses seem to register: each shock numbing our senses a little more in a progressive degeneration of our sensitivity. I prefer to take W H Davies's advice to find "time to stand and stare". I hope that my photographs will encourage the viewer to pause for thought.

Portfolio

1
Buttermere and Crummock Water
Silver sheets of water shine through the dusk,
reflecting the light of the setting sun.

2
Wastwater
Basking in a summer haze, embraces Illgill Head and
distances itself from the jagged crags of Great Gable.

3
Crummock Water
Gentle spring rain softens and subdues the gusty,
rippled surface of the lake and the fells rearing above it.

4
Buttermere
*Flashes a warning light before being obliterated
by a curtain of snow sweeping across the valley.*

5
Crummock Water
Drowsing in the evening calm, safe from the high altitude winds streaming out the 'mare's tail' clouds high above.

6
Ennerdale Water
Slowly stirs to wakefulness
in the dew-laden air at
the start of a warm
summer's day.

7

Ullswater

Shafts of winter sunlght
briefly brighten the scene,
but do nothing to warm
the dark troubled water.

8
Wastwater
Shimmers beneath the bulk
of England's highest
mountain, soon to be
baking under a hot summer
sun.

9
Loweswater

The windswept surface is ruffled by another squall as a searchlight shaft of light sweeps down across Holmwood.

10
Wastwater
Midsummer sun rises
above the head of the
valley, stirring the air into
surface-rippling currents.

11
Crummock Water
The sluggish surface
gleams with winter
sunlight, not sure what lies
ahead.

12
Derwentwater
*Its dark choppy surface
anticipating rougher
weather ahead as storm
clouds sweep out of
Borrowdale.*

13
Wastwater
Basking rocks, exposed by the summer's low water level, contentedly line the shore.

14
Bassenthwaite Lake
Writhes eerily in swirling
banks of mist.

15
Crummock Water
*The trappings of rural life
intrude into the quiet
stillness of the lake.*

16
Ennerdale Water
The waning light of evening still gives life to the water,
while the surrounding elements starts to slide into a deep slumber.

17
Bassenthwaite Lake
Dormant life undisturbed in winter stillness

18
Crummock Water
*The calmness of early
morning stays unruffled as
the sun feebly penetrates
the bank of cloud.*

19
Tewet Tarn
*Where ice has taken its
grip, the wind fails to stir
the surface.*

20
Crummock Water
*Rocks and stones abound
beneath the surface and,
when they succeed in
rising above the water,
some support vegetation.*

21
Buttermere
*The towering fells provide
its shelter and its
sustenance.*

22
Buttermere
*The stony bed of the lake
shows through the clear
water like a mosaic, but
still supports some plant
life in the shallows.*

23
Bassenthwaite Lake
Grasses appear to skate
across the wide expanse of
water under a big sky.

24
Buttermere
In misty mood. The winter
trees are soft and subdued
against a flat backdrop of
featureless fells.

25
Derwentwater
*Evening mists start to
gather at the end of a still
autumn day*

26
Buttermere
Its surface sparkling feebly
as a weak winter sun
filters through the stark
contorted branches of a
dormant tree.

27
Loweswater
Banks of mist give an air of unreality as they
separate the fells from their reflections.

28
Crummock Water
In sombre mood under the gathering clouds
of a winter storm.

29
Buttermere
*Shock waves seem to be
advancing down the lake as
the sky appears to explode
from Fleetwith Pike.*

30
Bassenthwaite Lake
*The rising sun burns off
the mist shrouding the lake
and swirling around
Scarness Point.*

31
Crummock Water
The sheep fence walking
into the water tries to close
off the view to Haystacks
and Great Gable.

32
Bassenthwaite Lake
*Peacefully reclines under
its canopy of branches as
Skiddaw loftily hides its
head in the clouds.*

33
Buttermere
Its guiding light showing the way to the end of the lake.

34
Derwentwater
*A flat calm provides poor
conditions for those with
sailing in mind.*

35
Crummock Water
*In harmony with a simple,
graceful group of grasses
on its shore.*

36
Loweswater
Lazes on a balmy summer's
morning, its surface dotted
with wildfowl.

37
Derwentwater
*With St Herbert's Island
looming out of the mist.*

38
Buttermere
*Its frozen surface an
abstract pattern of ice and
snow.*

39
Crummock Water
*The placid surface dotted
with dark rocks and spiky
reeds; Rannerdale Knotts
appearing to rise out of the
water like an island.*

40-42
Haweswater
*During times of drought, this artificially raised
lake reveals the ghosts of former habitation.*

43
St John's Common
*Bog pools form natural
reservoirs, slowing
drainage from the fells and
feeding becks, even in
times of drought.*

44
Buttermere
*A mooring post with
nothing to do in the winter
season.*

45 (above)
Crummock Water
*The boathouse lurking on the shore like some
amphibious reptile with mouth agape.*

46 (right)
Tilberthwaite
*The rock face of old mine workings draped with small
cascades of water, like strings of pearls.*

47
Crummock Water
*Fluctuating water levels
cause root growth
resembling the means of
mobility of a science fiction
monster.*

48
Bassenthwaite Lake
Shoreline trees partly submerged at times of flood.

49
Mellbreak Tarn
The incandescent heads of cotton grass
reflect darkly in the water.

50
Crummock Water
*Grassmoor's broken reflection
contrasts with sharp spikes of grass.*

51
Coledale Beck
The rushing water gathers
volume all the way as more
rivulets drain from the
bank.

52
Watendlath Tarn
Reeds mass together,
curving to touch the water
out of which they have
grown.

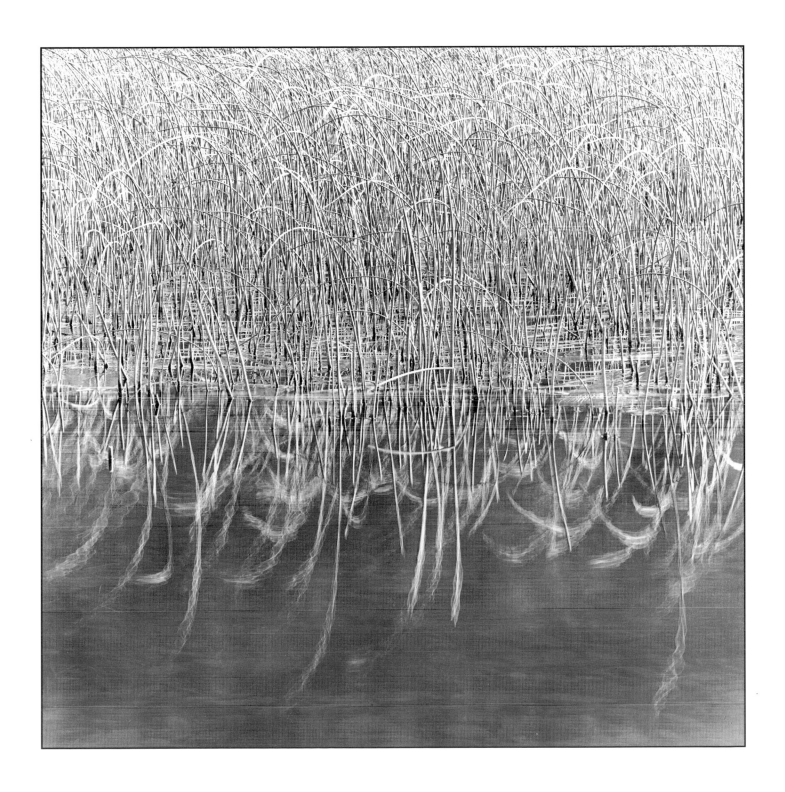

53
Red Tarn
*Floating grasses pattern
the surface like skaters'
tracks.*

54
Innominate Tarn
*Stalks and their reflections form
indecipherable hieroglyphics.*

55
Dock Tarn
*Nature's pen sketches out a delicate
pattern with these reeds.*

56
Wythburn Head Tarn
*Different reactions to wind
and currents fan these
grasses in all directions.*

57
Ennerdale Pool
*Water's edge grasses
become crystallised with
ice.*

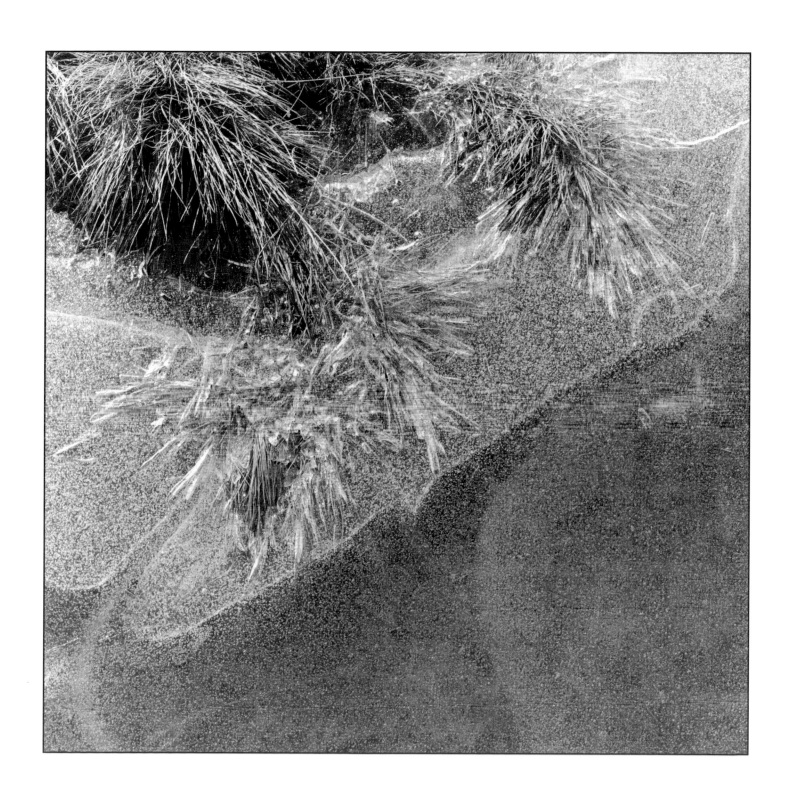

58
Frith Gill
Sticks and stones vainly
try to stop the rushing
water.

59
Watendlath Beck
*Miniature cascades, though
not so awesome, have all
the beauty of their big
brothers.*

60
Riddings Beck
*Water in both its liquid
and solid forms.*

61
Langdale Quarry
*Water softens the work of
man, just as it does with
any natural upheaval.*

62
Dash Falls
An icy curtain draws across the tumbling falls.

63
Dash Beck
Icicles swell and spread as they touch the moving water.

64
Gasgale Gill
The unending fight
continues as water in its
solid and liquid forms
makes a combined attack
on this rock.

65
Wyth Burn
Abruptly changes its placid mode to one of turbulence as its flow is interrupted.

66
Buttermere Moss
*In suspended animation,
columns of marsh gas
bubbles are temporarily
locked in a prison of ice.*

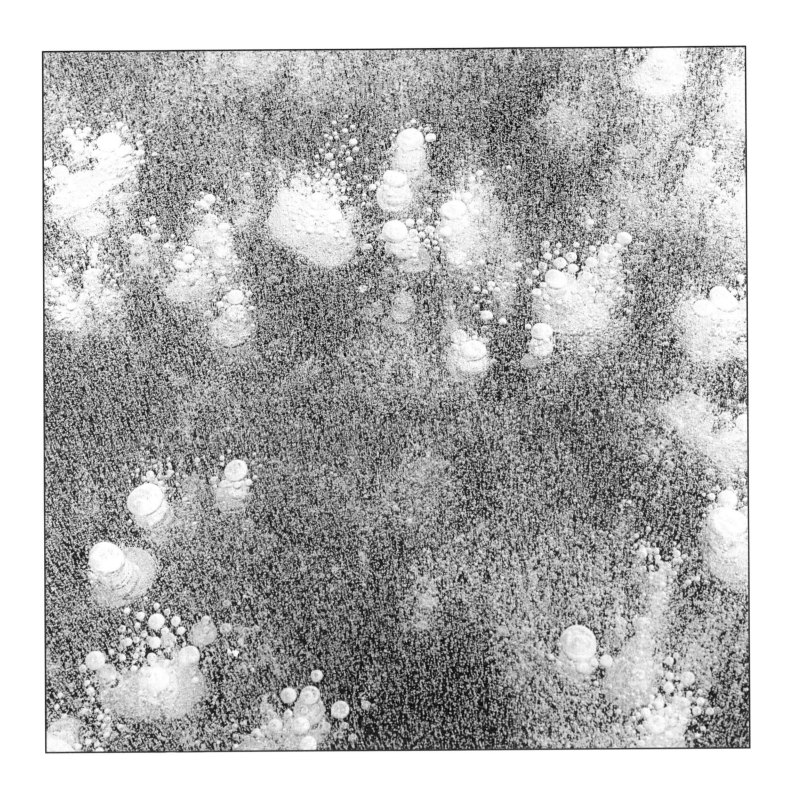

67
Mill Beck
*Exuding life and vitality as
it rushes and tumbles
down its rapid course.*

68
Skill Beck
Gleaming satin:
mysterious and beautiful.

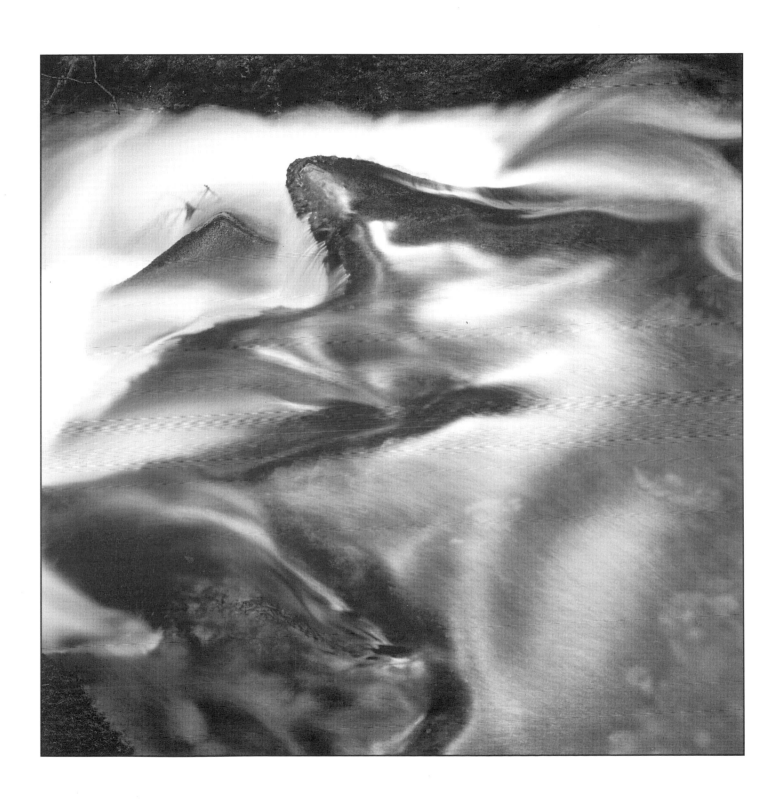

For a catalogue describing our full range of publications, please write to:
Creative Monochrome, 20 St Peters Road, Croydon, Surrey, CR0 1HD.